CONTENTS

Some words are shown in bold, **like this**. You can find out what they mean by looking in the glossary.

A bag of bones

Your skin covers your whole body, like a big stretchy bag. Your bones make up your skeleton, the solid framework that holds your body up, allows you to move, and stops you being a floppy pile on the ground. Your muscles lie underneath your skin. These connect to your bones.

A bag of numbers

You only have one suit of skin. It stretches all over your body. But you have lots of different muscles, some tiny and some large. You also have lots of different bones, of all different sizes. This book is going to take a look at some of the facts and figures to do with your skin, muscles, and bones.

Without your bones, you would be as floppy as a jellyfish! Your skin surrounds all your bones and muscles, protecting them.

Your skin and your bones together protect your body's vital **organs**. These are important body parts such as your heart, lungs, brain, and stomach.

Not just skin and bones

Your body is made up of a lot of different substances called **elements**. Elements can combine to make compounds. For example, water is a compound that is made up of two elements, hydrogen and oxygen.

Element	%
Oxygen	65
Carbon	18
Hydrogen	10
Nitrogen	3
Calcium	1.5
Phosphorous	1
Potassium	0.35
Sulphur	0.25
Sodium	0.15
Chlorine	0.15
Other	0.6

This table shows the percentages of different elements in the body.

Skin comes in a wide range of colours – but it all does the same job.

5

Skin deep

Your skin is your body's biggest organ. The other large organs in your body are your heart, liver, kidneys, stomach, and brain. An average adult's skin weighs about 3.6 kilograms (8 pounds). If it was all stretched out flat, it would cover around 2 square metres (22 square feet)!

Thin skin

Your skin is made of two main layers. The outer layer is called the epidermis. This is what you see when you look at your skin. The epidermis is covered in a layer of tough, dead **skin cells** that keep water and germs out. Most of the epidermis is very thin, only around 0.1 millimetre (0.003 inch) thick. Some parts of the epidermis are a lot thicker. For example, it can be up to 1.4 millimetres (0.06 inch) thick on the soles on the feet.

Thick skin

Rhinos have very tough, thick skin. The skin on a rhino's shoulders can be 45 millimetres (1.8 inches) thick. But there is a fish that can beat this! Whale sharks can have skin that is over 100 millimetres (3.9 inches) thick, giving them protection from the jaws of other sharks.

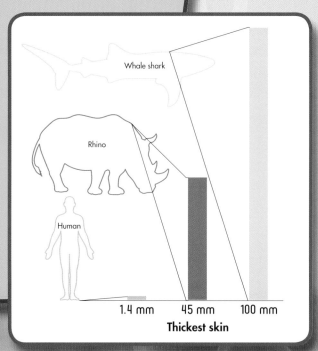

Whale shark

Rhino

Human

1.4 mm   45 mm   100 mm

Thickest skin

Getting under your skin

Lying below the epidermis is a layer called the dermis. It ranges from about 0.3 to 4 millimetres (0.01 to 0.16 inch) thick.

The dermis contains tiny **blood vessels** that bring blood to your skin. It also contains sweat ducts, where your sweat is made, and nerve cells. Nerve cells send signals from your skin to your brain – for example, when you touch something. The dermis also contains **hair follicles**, which your hairs grow from, and tiny muscles.

Shock, horror!

When you are frightened, your body releases a chemical called **adrenaline**. One of the things adrenaline does is make the tiny muscles in your skin contract (shorten), pulling the hair on your skin more upright. This makes little bumps on your skin, called goose pimples or goosebumps.

What does your skin do?

Your skin holds all your muscles, bones, organs, and other body parts together. It stops dirt, germs, and water getting into your body. It also stops water from leaking out of your body, so you don't dry up!

Your skin has the important job of protecting you against the Sun. The Sun sends out lots of different rays of light. Two of these different light types are called UVA (ultra-violet A) and UVB (ultra-violet B). When UVA and UVB rays hit your skin, your skin makes a dark chemical called melanin. Melanin absorbs the UV rays. Some dark skins already contain a lot of melanin, while some fair skins have very little.

Dark skin is much better at providing protection from the Sun's rays. This diagram shows the percentage of UVA and UVB rays that can get through pale skin and dark skin.

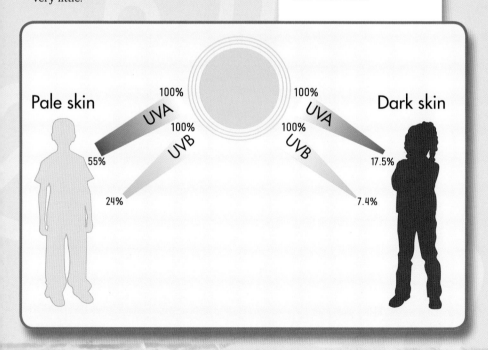

Pale skin

100% UVA
100% UVB
55%
24%

Dark skin

100% UVA
100% UVB
17.5%
7.4%

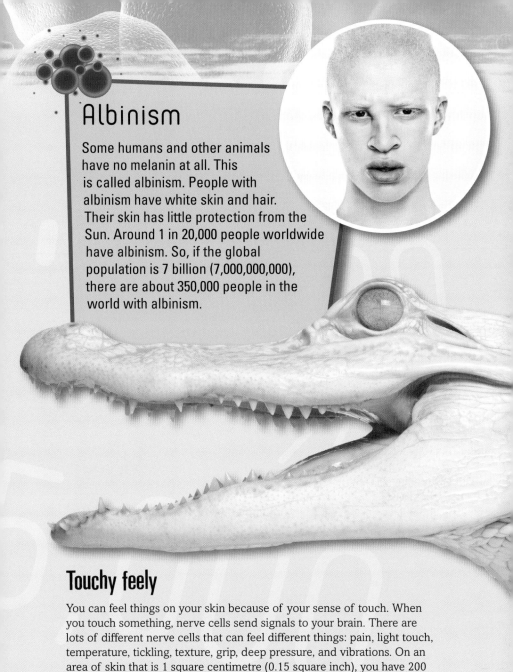

Albinism

Some humans and other animals have no melanin at all. This is called albinism. People with albinism have white skin and hair. Their skin has little protection from the Sun. Around 1 in 20,000 people worldwide have albinism. So, if the global population is 7 billion (7,000,000,000), there are about 350,000 people in the world with albinism.

Touchy feely

You can feel things on your skin because of your sense of touch. When you touch something, nerve cells send signals to your brain. There are lots of different nerve cells that can feel different things: pain, light touch, temperature, tickling, texture, grip, deep pressure, and vibrations. On an area of skin that is 1 square centimetre (0.15 square inch), you have 200 pain sensors, 15 pressure sensors, six cold sensors, and one heat sensor.

Warming up

Your body tries to keep its temperature at around 37 degrees Celsius (98.6 degrees Fahrenheit) in order for your organs to work properly. Other mammals, from your pet dog to a gorilla, need to keep warm too. When most mammals get cold, tiny muscles in the dermis contract. They pull the body hairs upright, which traps a layer of air close to the skin. This helps to keep the animal warm. It doesn't work very well for people, because we don't have enough hair. We just get goose pimples!

This table shows the normal body temperatures of some animals.

Animal	°C (°F)
Chicken	42.0 (107.6)
Goat	39.5 (103.1)
Pig	39.0 (102.2)
Sheep	39.0 (102.2)
Cow	38.5 (101.3)
Buffalo	38.2 (100.8)
Horse	38.0 (100.4)
Llama, alpaca	38.0 (100.4)
Human	37.0 (98.6)

Cooling down

When you get too hot, the tiny blood vessels in your skin expand. This allows more blood to flow into the skin. Since the skin is thin, the heat of the blood warms the air, which in turn cools you down. Your skin also releases sweat from the tiny sweat glands onto the skin's surface. This helps to cool you down further, as heat from your body makes the sweat **evaporate** – turn into a gas called water vapour.

Exercise can make you sweaty and red in the face. The redness is the blood rushing to the skin to cool it down.

Salty sweat

Sweat is about 95 per cent water, but it tastes salty because it contains chemicals called **minerals**, such as sodium. People doing sport or exercise often drink "sports drinks" that replace the minerals they lose, as well as the water, when they sweat a lot.

It is important to drink after exercise to replace the water you lose when you sweat.

Sweaty facts

- There are about three million little coiled sweat glands on the human body.
- It is usual to lose about one-third of a litre (two-thirds of a pint) every day, doing normal daily activities.
- A person doing exercise on a hot day can lose 2–3 litres (4.2–6.3 pints) every hour.
- If you uncurled a sweat gland, it would stretch over 1 metre (3 feet) long.

Changing skin

A baby's skin grows and stretches as the baby grows. Skin keeps growing through childhood and into adulthood. Even an adult's skin can grow if it needs to. For example, when a woman is pregnant, the skin over the belly area expands a lot to cover the bump. After the woman has had the baby, the skin can shrink back down.

New skin

Your skin is always renewing itself. New skin cells are made in the bottom of the epidermis. They push outwards and replace the old, dead skin cells. You have a totally new skin around every month, and you make about 1,000 skins in your lifetime!

Flake out

Every day, your skin sheds the outermost layer of dead skin cells on your body. About 30,000–40,000 skin cells flake off every minute! Over your lifetime, you will shed about 18 kilograms (40 pounds) of skin.

Make sure you buy new pillows from time to time. After being used for two years, about one-third of a pillow's weight is made up of dead skin cells, alive and dead **dust mites**, and dust mite poo!

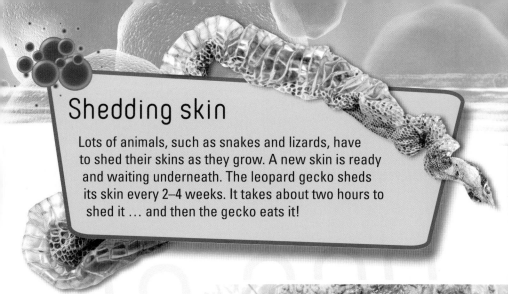

Shedding skin

Lots of animals, such as snakes and lizards, have to shed their skins as they grow. A new skin is ready and waiting underneath. The leopard gecko sheds its skin every 2–4 weeks. It takes about two hours to shed it … and then the gecko eats it!

Scabby skin

When your skin gets cut, it does an amazing job of healing itself. **Blood cells** rush to the area, and you bleed. Then some of the blood cells clump together to form a **blood clot**. This makes the bleeding stop. The clot hardens to form a scab. Below the scab the skin starts to repair itself. Once the new skin has grown over the wound, the scab falls off.

Scabs cover wounds and keep germs out.

Growing out of skin

Hairs grow out of the tiny hair follicles in your skin. You grow hair over all your body, except on the soles of your feet, the palms of your hands, and your lips. You have around five million hairs – the same number as a chimpanzee has! But most of the hairs on human bodies are too tiny and too fine to see.

Of course, you can see the hair on your head. But did you know that you lose around 80 hairs from your head every day? This may sound like a lot, but it doesn't make you look any different because you have about 100,000 hairs on your head. Human hair grows around 1 centimetre (0.4 inch) every month.

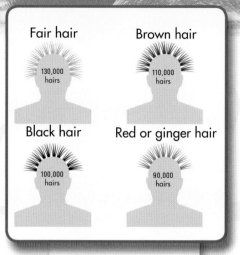

Fair hair
130,000 hairs

Brown hair
110,000 hairs

Black hair
100,000 hairs

Red or ginger hair
90,000 hairs

This diagram shows the average number of individual hairs on people with different hair colours. Each bunch represents 1,000 hairs.

Longest hair recorded	5.6 m (18.4 ft.)
Longest beard recorded	5.33 m (17.5 ft.)
Longest ear-hair recorded	18.1 cm (7.1 in.)

Here are some hair-raising records!

Furry hair

Lots of animals have thick fur to keep them warm. Sea otters have the thickest. In 6.5 square centimetres (1 square inch) on their skin, they grow 10 times as many hairs as you have on your whole head!

Hard as nails

Nails are made of the same material as hair. This material is called keratin. The nail root lies just below the skin, and it pushes layers of keratin out towards the fingertips. Fingernails grow about 2 millimetres (0.1 inch) every month. Toenails grow a bit slower. Both fingernails and toenails grow faster in hot weather.

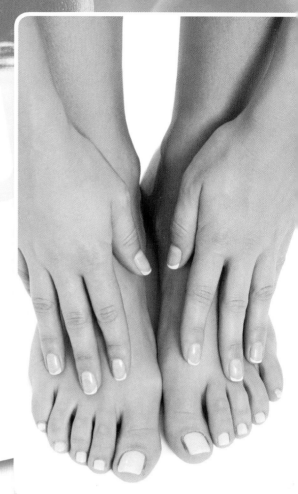

Nails protect the ends of your fingers and toes. Your fingernails provide your fingers with something to push against, so you can grip things. They also help you to deal with itches!

Fingerprints unchanged

Even though your skin renews itself around every month, you never lose the patterns in your fingerprints. Everyone – even identical twins – has a unique set of fingerprints. That means there are over seven billion different sets of fingerprints in the world!

Skin damage

The surface of your skin can be cut by something sharp, or scraped against something rough. But you can also damage your skin under the surface.

When something hits your skin hard, it can cause a bruise to form. This happens because the tiny blood vessels in your skin get damaged by the force of the hit, and they leak blood. But because the surface of the skin is not damaged, the blood can't leak out of the skin. So it pools under the surface of the skin, and you see this as a purplish bruise. Eventually the leaked blood breaks down and gets removed, and the bruise changes colour and fades away.

Bruises change colour over time before they fade away. This happens as your body breaks down the blood that leaked out when you got injured and reabsorbs it.

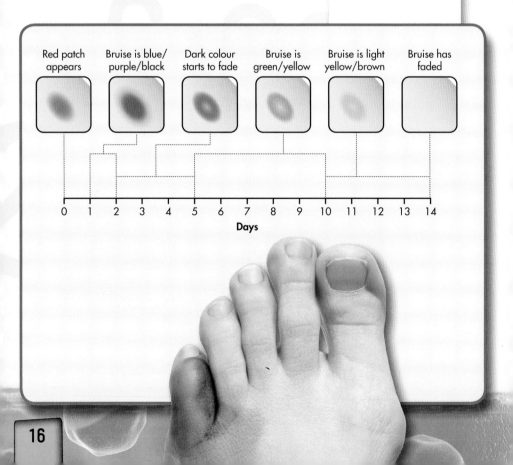

Red patch appears · Bruise is blue/purple/black · Dark colour starts to fade · Bruise is green/yellow · Bruise is light yellow/brown · Bruise has faded

0 1 2 3 4 5 6 7 8 9 10 11 12 13 14
Days

Ageing skin

As people get older, their skin starts to get wrinkles. Wrinkles happen because the skin becomes thinner, weaker, and less elastic with age. Places where the skin moves a lot, such as the face, become more wrinkled. The skin can't snap back to its original place as easily as it did when it was younger. The Sun's rays can also cause wrinkling – about 90 per cent of wrinkling on people over 20 is caused by the Sun.

Skin also becomes more fragile with age, so it is more likely to get damaged. It can tear and bruise more easily.

Compare the smooth skin of this baby with the wrinkled skin of her great-grandmother. Everyone's skin gets wrinkled as they age. The best way to slow down the appearance of wrinkles is to use sunscreen or to wear a sunhat!

Skin cancer

Skin **cancer** happens when skin cells grow abnormally – different from normal skin cells. These abnormal cells can grow into lumps on the skin, called tumours. There are different types of skin cancer. Some of them can spread to other parts of the body, and can kill people if they are not treated. Around the world, there are about 132,000 cases of skin cancer every year. But if the cancer is caught early and treated, many people recover.

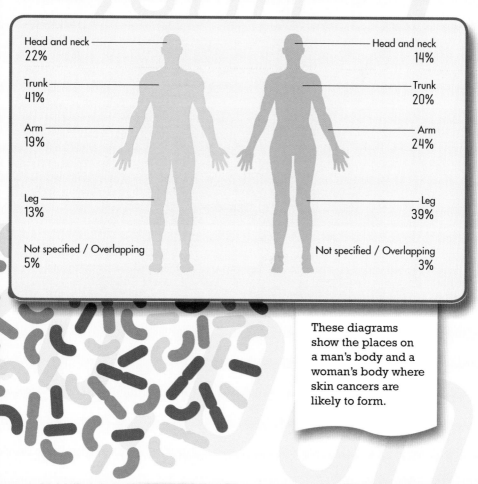

Head and neck
22%

Trunk
41%

Arm
19%

Leg
13%

Not specified / Overlapping
5%

Head and neck
14%

Trunk
20%

Arm
24%

Leg
39%

Not specified / Overlapping
3%

These diagrams show the places on a man's body and a woman's body where skin cancers are likely to form.

Viruses and bacteria

Viruses and **bacteria** are tiny living things that can invade your body and cause problems. Did you know that millions of bacteria live all over your skin all the time? Every 20 minutes, they double in number. But don't panic – every minute, about 25,000 of them float off on the flakes of skin that you shed.

Lots of different viruses can cause skin rashes. Measles and chicken pox are two common viruses that cause spots on the skin. Warts are hardened lumps of skin, usually found on the hands and feet. Warts are also caused by viruses. Certain kinds of bacteria can cause a condition called impetigo. This makes red sores and blisters appear on the infected parts of the skin.

Spots are caused when sweat, dead skin cells, and grease get trapped under the skin. Sometimes bacteria can infect them and make them worse.

Acne

Acne is a common skin problem for many teenagers. It causes lots of spots on the face, back, and chest. Around 80 per cent of people aged 11–30 will be affected by acne, but most will grow out of it. Only 5 per cent of women and 1 per cent of men over 25 have acne.

Many muscles

Just below your skin lie your muscles. They are responsible for making the movements all over your body. Many of them connect to bones, and some connect to other muscles. Some connect to your skin.

Expressive muscles

Your face has over 40 muscles! They don't all connect to bones. You use some of them to make your facial expressions. When you are happy, sad, worried, angry, or surprised, they push and pull the skin on your face to change how you look. You also use the muscles in your face to do other things, such as eating, sucking, blowing, drinking, whistling, and blinking.

You use muscles under the skin on your face to smile and to frown. Smiling uses about 17 muscles. Frowning uses a few more!

Busy muscles

There are two muscles in your face that are very busy – you use them about 30,000 times every day! They are the muscles that control your eyelids. Every time you blink, they shorten to pull your eyelids over your eyes.

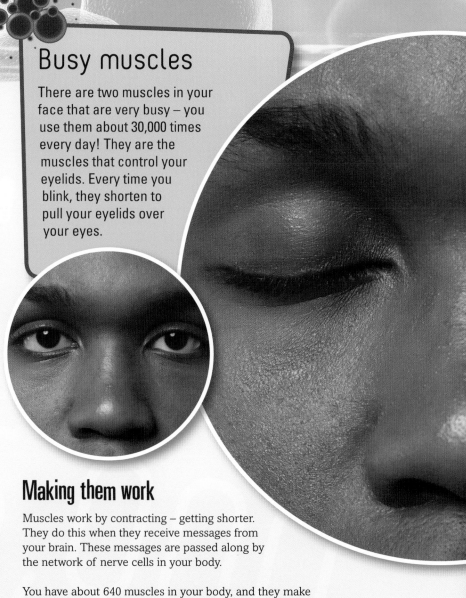

Making them work

Muscles work by contracting – getting shorter. They do this when they receive messages from your brain. These messages are passed along by the network of nerve cells in your body.

You have about 640 muscles in your body, and they make up about 40 per cent of your body weight. The shortest muscles are in your ears. They are only about 1 millimetre (0.04 inch) long. The longest muscles are in your thighs, and they are over 30 centimetres (12 inches) long. The biggest muscle in your body is in your bottom!

Muscle fibres

Muscles are made of bundles of thin threads called muscle fibres. Each muscle fibre is about as thin as a human hair. Large muscles are made up of several thousand muscle fibres.

Some people like to build up their muscles. They often have very little fat under their skin, so you can see the shapes of their muscles.

Muscles and moving

The muscles in your body that make your body move need to connect to your bones. These muscles are called skeletal muscles. They connect to your bones with tendons.

Tendons are strong, rope-like bits at the ends of muscles. They attach to your bones so that when your muscle contracts, it pulls on the tendon. This then pulls on the bone, and makes it move. There are about 4,000 tendons in the body.

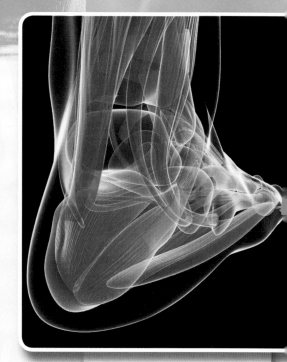

The thickest and strongest tendon in the body is the Achilles tendon. It connects the calf muscle to the heel. It can withstand 3–12 times the weight of the body when a person runs or jumps! But if your Achilles tendon gets damaged, you cannot walk.

Strong hands

Think how strong your fingers are. Rock climbers can hang off rock faces on only a couple of fingers! So why don't your hands and fingers look muscly? This is because the muscles that work the fingers are further up your arm. They are attached to the bones in your fingers by really long tendons.

Jigsaw of bones

Your bones give your body its shape and its structure. They allow your body to move around and support itself. Together, your bones make up your skeleton, which is about 15 per cent of your body's weight. Your skeleton can be split into two parts – the axial skeleton and the appendicular skeleton.

Support system

The axial skeleton forms your body's central support. It includes your skull, face, jaws, spine, ribs, and breastbone. Of the 206 bones in an adult body, 80 make up the axial skeleton. The appendicular skeleton is made of the parts that "hang off" the axial skeleton, including your shoulders, arms, hands, legs, and feet. It contains 126 of the 206 bones in the adult body.

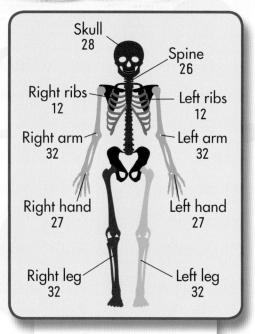

Skull
28

Spine
26

Right ribs
12

Left ribs
12

Right arm
32

Left arm
32

Right hand
27

Left hand
27

Right leg
32

Left leg
32

This diagram shows how many bones make up certain parts of the skeleton. The skull bones include three tiny bones in each ear.

Bone up on these facts!

Longest bone	Thigh (femur) – makes up about 25% of your height
Widest bone	Hip (**pelvis**) – widest part of the body
Smallest bone	Stirrup (stapes) – tiny ear bone, about 4 mm (0.16 in.) long

Loooooong neck

Giraffes have incredibly long necks so they can eat the leaves high on trees. You would think they have hundreds of neck bones. In fact, they have the same number as a human neck – seven! But each neck bone, or vertebra, can be over 25.4 centimetres (10 inches) long! Compare this to a human neck bone, which is about 10–15 millimetres (0.4–0.6 inch) long.

Fusing bones

A baby is born with about 300 bones. As the baby grows, some of these bones join together to get bigger and longer. They also get stronger. Adult bones are extremely strong. If you compare a piece of bone with a piece of steel that is the same weight, the bone will be six times stronger!

Ten skeletons

Like your skin, your bones renew themselves. Not every month, though! Every **bone cell** is renewed around every seven years. This means that in your lifetime you will grow a total of about 10 skeletons!

What is bone made of?

Your bones are not lifeless, dry, and flaky. They are alive and can bend slightly. They are made of millions of fibres called **collagen**, and minerals such as calcium. Calcium makes up around 70 per cent of your bones. Bones also have blood vessels, which bring nutrients and oxygen to the bones, and nerves that send messages to your brain.

Spongy bone

Blood vessels

Dry as a bone?

Like much of the human body, bones contain a lot of water. In fact, about 20 per cent of a bone's weight is water – that's the equivalent of about 2 litres (4.2 pints) in your body. Blood is about 92 per cent water and muscles are about 75 per cent water. Make sure you drink enough water!

Yellow bone marrow

Hard outer layer

Many bones have three layers. The centre is soft, jelly-like **bone marrow**. The middle layer is like a hard sponge. The outer layer is strong and solid.

Moving bones

Your muscles are what you use to move your bones. They are attached to your bones by tendons. Your bones act like levers. Just moving a muscle a few centimetres can produce a large movement at the end of the bone.

This diagram shows how a small movement of the **biceps** muscle in the arm can make a large movement of the hand.

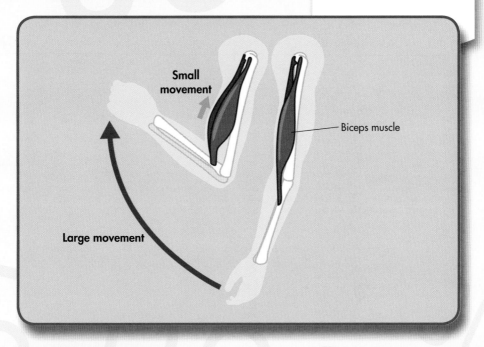

Small movement

Large movement

Biceps muscle

Protective bones

Bones don't just allow you to move. They provide protection for the soft, delicate parts of your body. Your skull protects your brain, and your ribs protect your heart and lungs. Your spine protects your spinal cord – this is the main bundle of nerves in your body that your other nerves branch off from.

Some animals don't have a bony skeleton inside their bodies. Instead, they have an exoskeleton. This is a hard case that surrounds the body and protects the organs inside. Crabs, beetles, and spiders are examples of animals with exoskeletons.

Blood factories

Bones have another job to do, apart from holding the body up, making movements, and protecting organs. They also do the important job of making new blood.

There are different kinds of blood cells in your blood – red blood cells carry oxygen around your body, and white blood cells fight germs and infections. Every minute, millions of these blood cells die and must be replaced. Luckily, your bone marrow makes around three million new blood cells every second!

How many blood cells?

One cubic millimetre (0.00006 cubic inch) of blood would fit into a tiny box that measured only 1 millimetre (0.039 inch) tall, by 1 millimetre (0.039 inch) wide, by 1 millimetre (0.039 inch) deep. In this tiny box of blood, there would be thousands of white blood cells and millions of red ones!

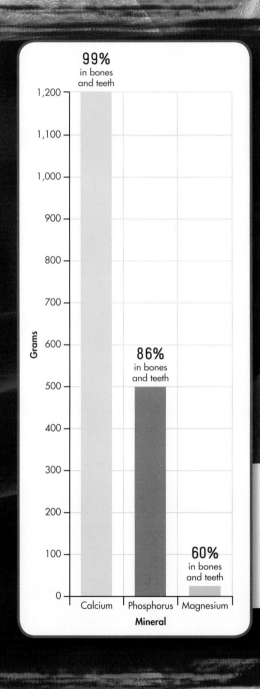

99%
in bones
and teeth

86%
in bones
and teeth

60%
in bones
and teeth

Grams

1,200
1,100
1,000
900
800
700
600
500
400
300
200
100
0

Calcium   Phosphorus   Magnesium

Mineral

Mineral stores

Your bones can store important minerals for your body, such as iron and calcium. Your body usually gets enough of these minerals from the food you eat, but if your diet is poor your body uses the minerals stored in the bone. When your diet gets better again, the mineral stores get topped back up.

This bar chart shows the amount of the minerals calcium, phosphorus, and magnesium that are in the body. It also shows the percentage of each that is found in the bones and teeth.

Cartilage

Not every part of the human skeleton is made of bone. Some bits are made from a lighter, softer, bendier material called **cartilage**.

Your nose is made of cartilage – try wobbling and squashing it. You wouldn't be able to do this if it was made of bone. Your ears are also made of cartilage, and you have cartilage where your ribs join the breastbone down the front of your chest. Your spine is made of lots of bones called vertebrae, and in between these vertebrae are pads of cartilage. Like many body parts, cartilage is mostly made of water – around 85 per cent is water.

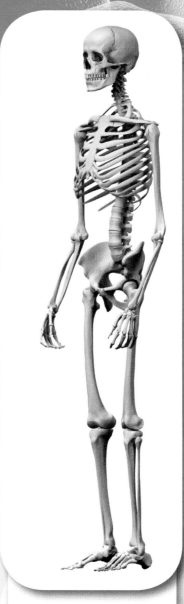

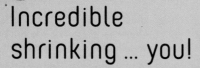

Incredible shrinking ... you!

You are taller in the morning, when you get out of bed, than you are in the afternoon and the evening. As you go about your daily life, the cartilage in your spine squashes down a bit. An adult loses an average of 15 millimetres (0.6 inch) in height during the day! As you sleep, your spine stretches out again.

Cartilage is not as strong or as long-lasting as bone. This is why you never see noses and ears on the skulls of dead people. The cartilage dries up and breaks off, leaving a gap where the nose was and a head without ears!

Cartilage becomes bone

When babies are born, most of their bones are made out of cartilage. As they grow, it hardens and turns to bone. By the age of 25, most of the skeleton is made of bone, apart from the parts that never become bone, such as the nose and ears.

No bones

A shark's skeleton is made from 100 per cent cartilage. This helps the shark to stay afloat, because cartilage is lighter than bone. Most other fish have swim bladders (pouches inside their bodies that contain air) to help them float, but sharks don't. Cartilage can bend more than bone too, so sharks are very flexible.

Joining up

Most of your bones are joined to other bones. Only one of the 206 bones in an adult body is completely floating – this is the hyoid bone in the front part of the neck. The rest are joined by joints. There are over 200 joints in the body. Most of them allow for some movement between the bones, so the body can bend, turn, and twist.

Oil for joints

Joints need lubrication – something to keep them moving smoothly, just like car engines need oil. Joints are surrounded by a liquid called synovial fluid, which keeps them moving smoothly. Each knee joint contains about 7 millilitres (0.4 cubic inch) of synovial fluid, contained inside a bag called a joint capsule.

Fixed joints

Some joints don't allow any movement of the bones they connect. For example, your skull is made up of several bones joined together. These joints are called sutures. There are also sutures in your pelvis – a group of bones that forms a ring near the base of the spine.

Different joints

There are various different kinds of joints in your body, other than sutures. They have different names – hinge joint, ball and socket joint, saddle joint, gliding joint, and pivot joint. They move in different ways and allow different amounts of movement between the bones they connect.

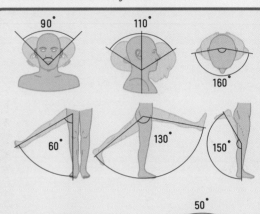

This diagram shows the normal amount of movement that different kinds of joints can make.

Twit-twoo!

One of the biggest movements your body can make is turning your head around from one side to the other – you can turn it through 160 degrees. Owls, however, can turn their heads through 270 degrees! They have twice as many neck bones as humans.

Cushioning the blow

Most joints have a pad of cartilage between the bones they connect. This provides a squashy cushion and stops the bones from grinding against each other. There are 23 discs of cartilage in the spine.

In the knee joints, the ends of the leg bones are covered in cartilage. The cartilage acts as a shock absorber, and can cope with the high impacts that people put on their knees. Knee cartilage can take up to 7 tonnes of force before it snaps – that's more than the weight of an elephant!

Coping with pressure

Your knee joints have to cope with a lot of pressure from the weight of your body and the movements you make with your knees. An average adult weighs about 70 kilograms (150 pounds). Simply standing on one leg puts almost all of this weight force onto one knee. But if you add in movement, direction, and speed, such as when you are climbing, running, or jumping, the force on your knees increases a lot.

This diagram shows the amount of pressure on one knee joint when a person is standing on one leg, climbing, and jumping. Each figure represents the weight of one person.

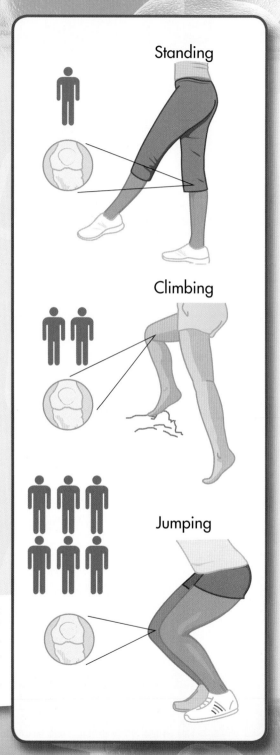

Standing

Climbing

Jumping

All bound up

Joints need to be stable in order to work properly. This means that they should not wobble about. All the bones, muscles, and tendons need to be in the right places. They are all held in place by tough bands of tissue called ligaments. Ligaments can be twice as strong as a nylon rope! They stop the bones from moving too far and damaging the joint.

Double-jointed

People who are "double-jointed" don't actually have double joints. It just means their ligaments are super-stretchy and so they can move their joints further than most people can.

Putting it all together

Joints work with bones, muscles, tendons, and ligaments to make you move around. It is amazing how many things need to combine to do even the simplest movement. For example, turning a page in a book uses about 40 muscles in your hand and fingers, the 32 bones in your arm, and all the tendons and ligaments that connect the muscles and bones. Throwing a ball involves more than 60 bones, 50 joints, and 100 muscles!

Think of all the movements a javelin thrower makes during a throw. Many different bones, muscles, tendons, and ligaments are involved.

Controlling the movements

Most of the movements you make are controlled by a part of your brain called the **motor centre**. It sends out signals called **nerve impulses**. These travel down nerve cells to your muscles. There, the nerve cells join to your muscles with lots of tiny branches called motor end plates. The impulses make your muscles contract. This pulls on the tendons attached to your bones, and so your bones move. The nerve impulses from your brain can travel up to 435 kilometres (270 miles) per hour!

Skin, bones, muscles, tendons, ligaments, and joints work together to make movements. The speed of an animal's movements depends on the strength and size of the muscles involved and the way the animal's body is put together.

Animal	Speed: km/h (mph)	Acceleration: m/s^2 (ft./s^2)
Cheetah	104.5 (65)	10.2 (33)
Lion	80.0 (50)	9.5 (31)
Gazelle	80.0 (50)	4.5 (15)
Human	43.6 (27)	3.5 (11.4)
Elephant	40.0 (25)	0.4 (1.3)

This table shows the top running speeds for humans and some other animals. It also shows how quickly they can accelerate (increase their speed). With an acceleration of 10.2 metres (33 feet) per second per second (/s^2), the cheetah is definitely the quickest off the mark. It is also the fastest!

Bone and joint problems

Have you ever broken a bone? Many children break a bone – sometimes more than one! In fact, through childhood, 42 per cent of boys and 27 per cent of girls suffer from a broken bone. Most of these broken bones – 85 per cent of them – happen to children over five years old. Younger children have softer, bendier bones that are less likely to break.

Snap!

When a bone is broken, blood leaks out from the blood vessels in the bone and starts to clump together to form a blood clot. After a few days, a network of bone fibres starts to form, filling the gap in the bone. Around two weeks later, soft spongy bone grows around these fibres. After two or three months, hard bone has formed – the bone is strong again!

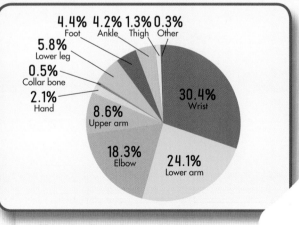

This pie chart shows which bones children are most likely to break.

Record bone-breaker!

Evel Knievel, a motorbike stuntman, is listed in *Guinness World Records* as the person with the most broken bones in a lifetime. By the time he was 37, Knievel had suffered a total of 433 bone fractures!

Bone disease

Some people have conditions that affect their bones. Brittle bone disease (otherwise known as osteogenesis imperfecta) causes people's bones to be brittle and easily broken. Around one baby in every 30,000 is born with brittle bone disease. Some of these babies suffer fractures – cracks in bones – even before they are born.

Leukaemia and myeloma

Leukaemia and myeloma are both types of cancer
that affect the bone marrow. When people have leukaemia,
the bone marrow starts to release white blood cells that
are not quite ready to be released into the blood. This
upsets the delicate balance of red blood cells in the blood.
It also means that people can't fight infections very well,
as their white blood cells don't work properly.

Myeloma affects **plasma cells** in the bone marrow.
It causes bone pain and fractures, and also makes
people less able to fight infections.

This bar chart
shows the
number of men
and women
out of 100,000
that die from
myeloma in
different areas
of the world.

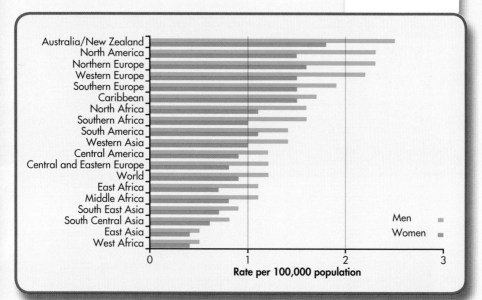

Australia/New Zealand
North America
Northern Europe
Western Europe
Southern Europe
Caribbean
North Africa
Southern Africa
South America
Western Asia
Central America
Central and Eastern Europe
World
East Africa
Middle Africa
South East Asia
South Central Asia
East Asia
West Africa

Men
Women

0   1   2   3

Rate per 100,000 population

Children with leukaemia

The good news for children with leukaemia is that
with good treatment, over 85 per cent will live for
more than five years after the leukaemia has been
diagnosed. Living for more than five years means
that the disease is very unlikely to return.

Painful joints

Arthritis is a common condition that causes painful and swollen joints. Around 10 million people in the UK have a type of arthritis.

There are two main types. Osteoarthritis causes the cartilage in the joints to wear away. Rheumatoid arthritis causes the joints to become sore and swollen, and the cartilage starts to break down.

This X-ray picture shows a hand affected by osteoarthritis, the most common form of joint disease. The cartilage between the joints in the finger bones has worn away.

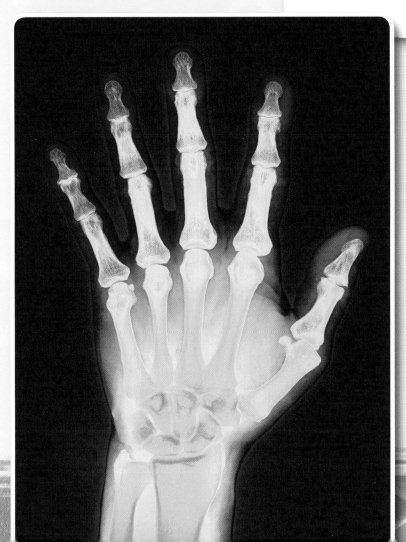

Not all skin and bones

So, your skin and your bones work together with your muscles, your tendons, and your ligaments. They help to make your movements and your expressions. Your skin is your ever-renewing coat that protects your whole body and is your first line of defence against germs. It stops you from drying out and protects you from the Sun. Your bones make the framework that supports your whole body and protects your precious organs.

What colour?

Although polar bears have white fur, and blend in perfectly to their snowy surroundings, they actually have black skin. Chameleons have amazing skin that can change colour, depending on the temperature and the mood of the chameleon. If a chameleon is scared or angry, the skin becomes bright green. If the chameleon is hungry or cold, it turns brown or yellowish.

Keep them fit!

You need to make sure you eat the right food in order to keep your skin and bones healthy. There are five food groups, and different foods have different amounts of these things:

- carbohydrates – these give you energy to move around
- fats – these also give you energy, and they transport nutrients around your body
- proteins – these build and repair muscles
- vitamins – these build skin, cartilage, tendons, and bones
- minerals – these build bones and teeth.

Look after your body by eating well and doing some exercise. Exercise keeps your bones strong and your joints and muscles flexible and strong.

Test yourself!

Take a look at the questions below. You will find all the answers somewhere in this book. Check out the pages where the information is if you need reminding of the answers.

1 How much sweat might a person exercising on a hot day lose?
a   0.5–1 litre (1–2.1 pints)
b   2–3 litres (4.2–6.3 pints)
c   4–5 litres (8.5–10.6 pints)

2 Which hormone causes your skin to have goose pimples or goosebumps?
a   insulin
b   oestrogen
c   adrenaline

3 Lots of body parts contain water. Put these in order, from the one containing the largest percentage of water to the one containing the smallest.
cartilage; bones; blood; muscles

4 If you weigh 50 kilograms (110 pounds), and your skeleton weighs 7.5 kilograms (16.5 pounds), what percentage of your body weight is made up of your bones?
a   10%
b   12%
c   15%

5 If you have 10 million bacteria living on your skin, and an hour later there are 80 million, how long does it take for the bacteria to double in number?
a   5 minutes
b   20 minutes
c   45 minutes

6 Which five body parts from the list below are organs?
hand; skin; liver; hair; heart; stomach; knee; mouth; brain; biceps; tendon

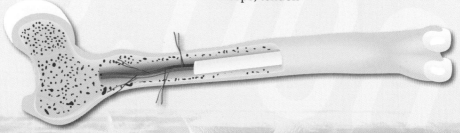

7 How many of the 206 bones in your body are not connected to other bones by joints?

a   1
b   21
c   41

8 How many muscles are there in your face?

a   over 40
b   over 100
c   over 120

9 Over how much of your skin do you have 200 pain sensors, 15 pressure sensors, six cold sensors, and one heat sensor?

a   1 square centimetre (0.15 square inch)
b   0.5 square metre (5.4 square feet)
c   your whole body

10 How many skin cells flake off your body every minute?

a   300–400
b   3,000–4,000
c   30,000–40,000

Nosy animal!

There is a strange animal with a star-shaped nose that lives underground and has a poor sense of sight. Its nose has 22 fleshy "tentacles" that are incredibly sensitive to touch. This nose is only about 1 centimetre (0.4 inch) wide, but it has around 100,000 touch receptors. A human hand has only 17,000! This super-sensitive nose can detect worms and insects moving about in the ground. Do some research to find out which creature this strange nose belongs to.

Answers:
1b; 2c; 3: blood (92%), cartilage (85%), muscles (75%), bones (20%); 4c; 5b; 6: skin, liver, heart, stomach, brain; 7a; 8a; 9a; 10c

Glossary

adrenaline chemical that your body releases when it responds to certain situations, such as being frightened

bacteria tiny living things that you can't see, but that live on and in your body. Some types of bacteria are harmless, while others can cause illnesses and disease.

biceps large muscle at the front of the arm, above the elbow, that contracts to bend the elbow

blood cell tiny building block that makes up your blood. Red blood cells carry oxygen, and white blood cells protect against bacteria and viruses.

blood clot sticky lump of blood cells that forms where a blood vessel is cut, to stop blood from leaking out

blood vessel any of the tubes in the body that blood flows through, from tiny capillaries to large veins and arteries

bone cell tiny building block that makes up all the bones in your body

bone marrow fatty substance in the bone, in which blood cells are made

cancer disease that causes certain cells in the body to grow abnormally

cartilage tough white tissue that forms part of the skeleton of humans and other animals

collagen tough fibres made of chemicals called proteins

dust mite tiny living animal, related to spiders, that feeds on flakes of human skin

element substance that cannot be broken down into simpler substances, but can combine with other elements to make more complex substances called compounds

evaporate turn from a liquid into a gas. Evaporation is usually caused by heating the liquid.

hair follicle small sac that surrounds the root of every hair, with a narrow hole that the hair grows out from

mineral substance formed in the Earth's crust

motor centre part of your brain that deals with movement in your body

nerve impulse signal that moves along a stimulated nerve fibre and triggers an action

organ part of your body that performs a particular task; for example, your heart is an organ that pumps blood around your body

pelvis group of bones that forms a ring near the base of the spine and includes the hip bones

plasma cell tiny building block that makes up the clear, liquid part of blood. Red and white blood cells travel in the plasma.

skin cell tiny building block that makes up your skin

virus tiny living thing that can enter your body and cause illness and disease

Find out more

BOOKS

Bones (Body Focus), Carol Ballard (Heinemann Library, 2009)

The Everything Kids' Human Body Book, Sheri Amsel (Adams Media, 2012)

Human Body: A Children's Encyclopedia (DK Reference), Richard Walker et al. (Dorling Kindersley, 2012)

WEBSITES
www.bbc.co.uk/schools/gcsebitesize/pe/appliedanatomy/2_anatomy_skeleton_rev1.shttml
This BBC website is full of information about bones and joints.

kidshealth.org/kid/htbw/bones.html
Here you can find out lots of information about bones, and there are diagrams to click on and find out more.

The same website also has a section all about skin:
kidshealth.org/kid/htbw/skin.html

And another section all about muscles:
kidshealth.org/kid/htbw/muscles.html

www.sciencekids.co.nz/gamesactivities/movinggrowing.html
There is a game on this website where you have to drag the correct name to the correct bone.

www.wartgames.com/themes/humanbody/skeleton.html
There are links to lots of different bone-based games on this website.

FURTHER RESEARCH
You could visit your local library to see if there are any books about skin, muscles, and bones. You could also do some research to find out how athletes keep their bones and muscles strong and their joints flexible. You could investigate which types of food benefit the skin most.

Index

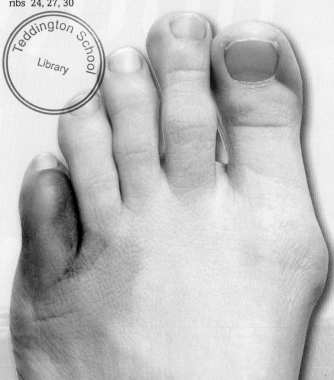